Java Boot

Learn the Basics of Java Programming in 2 Weeks

More Free and Bargain Books at
__KindleBookSpot.com__

Table Of Contents

Introduction

I want to thank you and congratulate you for downloading the book, *"Learn the Basics of Java Programming in 2 Weeks"*.

This book contains proven steps and strategies in learning the basics of Java programming in two weeks. You should be able to create simple programs after reading this book, or while learning it as you apply the things that you have learned while coding your program.

It is important that you have basic computer knowledge before jumping to Java programming. It also helps if you know other programming language as well. You can design one program flow and use it in different programming languages. It's like writing a novel in English language and translating it to different languages. However, there is a reason why a programmer chooses a particular programming language for the designed program flow. You can say that each programming language has a distinct feature that a programmer needs for the output that he has in mind.

Java has many uses, and it is not difficult to learn it. When learning a programming language, it is always easier to learn by example. Expect to see lots of sample programs in this tutorial, and expect that you will do some on your own. You will be provided with the output so you will know if you did it right.

The basic Java programming syntax will be provided in this book as well as the list of reserved words that you should avoid using as variable name.

You will be more than glad that you picked this book for your Java programming basic learning.

Thanks again for downloading this book, I hope you enjoy it!

Chapter 1: Welcome to the World of Java Programming

Java is considered a high-level programming language designed to create powerful, secure applications. It runs on various platforms or operating systems, like Windows, Mac OS X, Linux, and several versions of UNIX. Java is a programming language known for its flexibility, maintainability, and scalability.

First, you need to install Java in your computer. As stated in the introduction of this ebook, you need to have basic computer knowledge. It also helps a lot if you are familiar with a particular programming language or Java.

A Bit of Java History

James Gosling founded Sun Microsystems. In June 1991, Gosling began the Java language project. It was initially called Oak, and then Green. In the end, it was named Java for no particular reason. Java 1.0 was released in 1995. The current Java Standard Edition is Java SE8.

On 2007, Java's core code was released as free and open source software, apart from a tiny segment of code that Sun had no copyright.

Java has Several Advantages

Java is object-oriented, which means that everything is an object when it comes to Java. It can be extended with ease.

It is also considered platform independent, unlike most programming languages such as C and C++. When you compile Java, you don't compile it into platform-specific machine; rather you compile it into byte code. The said byte code is disseminated over the web and a virtual machine interprets it.

Java is simple, it is easy to learn. However, it is best for you to have a deeper understanding of the concepts of Object Oriented Programming (OOP) so it will be easier for you to master Java. One of the main advantages of object-oriented programming over procedural programming is its ability to let a programmer create different modules that don't need modifications even if he adds a new type of object. You will understand more of it when you enhance your knowledge regarding OOP while you learn Java programming.

Java has secure features; it has the ability to help you create a tamper-free, virus-free system.

The Java compiler can generate an architectural-neutral object file format. The compiled code is executable on many processors with Java runtime system. This also makes Java portable.

Java is dynamic; many programmers believe that it is actually more dynamic than C++ or C. Java can effectively adapt to any environment.

There are more advantages of Java, and you will discover them all as you learn Java programming and gain further knowledge regarding the beauties of OOP.

Things that you will Need to Start your Journey into the World of Java Programming

You need a computer powered at least by an Intel Core2Duo processor, and has a minimum of 1GB of RAM. These are actually the most basic, if not lower, specs of most computers you can buy today. If you can play videogames on your computer then it has more than enough power for Java programming.

Your Operating System (OS) should be Windows XP, Windows 7, Windows 8, or Linux. This book has provided the set up paths for the said platforms, although it is recommended to use the provided link for online coding to get your started immediately.

You need to choose Java JDK8 if you choose to install Java in your computer.

You also need to get Microsoft Notepad or other text editor.

Local Environment

If you would like to create a local environment set up for your Java programming, then you need to go download java for free, make sure to choose the version that is compatible with your OS.

After choosing the right Java for your OS, follow the instructions to download Java properly and run the ".exe" file that will allow you to install Java in your computer. Once installed, you need to set the path for your particular platform.

The Path for Windows

Let us assume that you have successfully installed Java in your computer, it looks like this when you try to view the directory:

c:\Program Files\java\jdk

Point your cursor on 'My Computer' and click on it. Once you have opened it, right-click on it and choose 'Properties' (located at the bottom part of the choices).

Under the 'Advanced' tab you will see a button that says 'Environment variables', you need to click on it.

You need to modify the 'Path' variable next. It needs to contain the path to Java.exe. If your current path is set to:

C:\WINDOWS\SYSTEM32, you need to change the path to read:

C:\WINDOWS\SYSTEM32;c:\Program Files\java\jdk\bin

The Path for Linux, UNIX, Solaris, FreeBSD

You need to set the environment variable PATH to properly point the location where the Java binaries are installed. You can refer to your shell documentation if you encounter some trouble setting the path.

If you use 'bash', for example, then you need to add 'export PATH=/path/to/java: $PATH', it would appear like this:

.bashrc: export PATH=/path/to/java:$PATH

The Popular Java Editors

The programming languages in the past did not need text editors, unlike most modern programming languages, but you need to use one for Java programming. There are several sophisticated IDEs (Integrated Development Environment) that you can use for your Java programming. IDE is a software application that presents or gives comprehensive facilities for software creation or development that programmers can use. IDE typically consists of build automation tools, debugger, and text editor.

Here are some of the most popular text editors that you can use:

1. Notepad – if your computer runs on Windows, then you can use the built-in Notepad editor to write your code.

2. Netbeans - is actually a Java IDE that you can download free from this
http://netbeans.org/index.html

3. Eclipse - is another Java IDE that is created by the eclipse open-source community.

Once you have everything ready, we can proceed to learning the basics of Java programming that can take you closer to your goal of creating a Java program all on your own.

Chapter 2: "Hello Java", the First Encounter

The "Hello" program is the first lesson that beginners at programming learn, and for so many reasons. The program introduces you to the first things that you need to do first to begin coding your program as well as some of the syntax that you need to learn and use.

For the samples, we will use the online coding (the link was provided earlier) for uniformity. You can use your own Java.exe later. The actual online Java console presents different font colors. We will only use different color fonts in our sample if there is certain command or character / symbol that must be explained in details.

Hello Java, the Basic Syntax

Take a look at the sample program below and we will analyze is line by line:

```
1    public class FirstProgram {

2

3      /* This is the first sample.

4       * We will print 'Hello Java' as the output

5       */

6

7      public static void main(String []args) {

8          System.out.println("Hello Java"); // prints Hello Java

9      }

10   }
```

By the way, it is extremely important to keep in mind that Java is case sensitive. The identifier 'Hello' and 'hello' are not the same when it comes to Java programming. Make sure to define everything correctly and use the identifiers in their right cases consistently throughout the program.

The first line bears the class name 'FirstProgram'; do not put spaces in between the words that make up the class name. The first letter of the next word, that's included in the class name, should be in upper case. Your program should always begin with 'public class' (all in lower case) followed by the class name. Do you see the yellow bracket at the end of the class name? Don't forget to include it as well. It serves as a mark that the things after it are the code of your program.

Your program file name should bear the same name that you assigned as class name. When saving the file name, just add '.java' after the file name. Take a look at the example above. When you save it, write 'FirstProgram.java'.

The second line is empty to make the codes more readable.

The third line starts with '/*', and on the fifth line you have '*/'. You use them when you need to include a multi-line comment, which the compiler will not treat as part of the program. You usually include comments to explain a little about the program, a sort of reminder to yourself or to help the programmer assigned to maintain the program.

The seventh line contains the method name, and all the method names should be written in lower case. The method name is always written like this:

public static void main(String []args) {

The bracket at the end of the method name prompts the program to do everything enclosed within the brackets (in our example the closing bracket is found in line 9).

In the example, line 8 contains a command that tells the program to print 'Hello Java' on screen. There should be a semi colon (;) at the end of the command sentence. The '//' symbol is another comment, and it is the symbol to use if you only need to make a single line comment.

The '.println' is the command that tells the program to print the ones inside the parentheses.

Make sure that each beginning bracket has a closing bracket. In the example, the beginning bracket in line 1 has closing bracket in line 10. The beginning bracket in line 7 has closing bracket in line 9.

Here's another:

```
1  public class FirstName {

2      public static void main(String []args) {
3          System.out.println("Erika");
4      }
5
```

It will yield this result:

Also, make sure to indent properly to make the codes more readable.

You will learn more about the data types and variables in the next chapter.

Chapter 3: Data Types and Variables

In this chapter, you will learn about the different data types that you will work on, as well as assigning value to a variable. You will also learn the reserved words that you should not use as variable name.

The Integer (*int*)

An integer is either a positive or negative number. Zero is also considered an integer.

int is short for integer in Java programming, and you will know its use later. You don't need to enclose the integer in quotes if you want to print it.

Take a look at this program:

```
1   public class IntPrinting {

2       public static void main(String []args) {
3           System.out.println(10);
4       }
5   }
```

It will yield this result:

```
10
```

The *int* data type can only accept the values between -2,147,483,648 and 2,147,483,647.

Any number that you put inside the parentheses of 'System.out.println();' will be printed, as long as you follow the correct syntax like the given example.

The Boolean (***true*** or ***false***)

A *boolean* data type can only be either true or false. It won't yield any other answer. You don't need to put it in quotes because the program recognizes *true* and *false* as the legitimate value for *boolean*.

Take a look at the sample program:

```
1  public class BooleanPrinting {

2    public static void main(String []args) {
3      System.out.println(true);
4    }
5  }
```

It will yield this result:

```
True
```

Try replacing *true* inside the parentheses with 'me', like this:

```
1   public class BooleanPrinting {

2     public static void main(String []args) {
3       System.out.println(me);
4     }
5   }
```

It will yield this result:

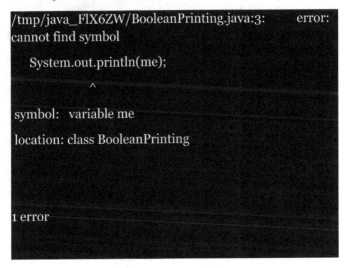

```
/tmp/java_FlX6ZW/BooleanPrinting.java:3:       error:
cannot find symbol
    System.out.println(me);
                       ^
 symbol:   variable me
 location: class BooleanPrinting


1 error
```

It does not recognize the word 'me' because it is a string. When printing strings, you need to write it within the quotes.

The Character (**char**)

The character or *char* data type represents a single character. All values must be enclosed in single quotes; otherwise you will get an error message.

Take a look at the sample below:

```
1  public class BooleanPrinting {

2    public static void main(String []args) {
3      System.out.println('r');
4    }
5  }
```

It will give this result:

```
r
```

The *int, boolean*, and *char* are Java's basic data types. You will encounter more of them later.

Using Variables

You can store a value to a variable in Java programming, and other programming languages have such feature as well. When you use a variable in Java, you need to specify the data type.

Here is the list of the Java reserved words that you should not use as variables:

abstract	assert	boolean	break	long
byte	case	catch	char	private
class	const	continue	default	short
do	double	else	enum	switch
extends	final	finally	float	native
for	goto	if	implements	new
import	instanceof	int	interface	package
transient	protected	public	return	super
synchronized	static	strictfp	throws	this
volatile	while	try	throw	void

Remember that you should not begin your variable in upper case, although you can use upper case within the variable name like this:

int myFavoriteNumber = 10;

You need to write *int* in the beginning to identify the data type, 'myFavoriteNumber' is the variable name, and '10' is the value assigned to it.

Try this on your own:

1. The *int* variable mySampleNumber must be equal to 6.

2. The *boolean* variable mySampleAnswer must be equal to *true*.

   1. The *char* variable mySampleLetter must be equal to L.

Just assign each variable the value that the instruction tells you to assign. When you run the program you won't see the values printed onscreen. If you want to print the values, then you need to add System.out.println() in your program, how will you do it? Hint – each variable that you need to print must have its own System.out.println(), make sure to write the correct one and it should not be the real value of the variable.

Just this once, you need to add these lines to your program:

```
8      System.out.println(mySampleNumber);

9      System.out.println(mySampleAnswer);


10     System.out.println(mySampleLetter);
```

You will get this output:

```
6

true

L
```

Now you're ready for a more challenging, yet fulfilling lessons.

Chapter 4: Useful Tables, Keep them Handy

This chapter contains the different tables that you need to keep handy because they serve as your quick reference in learning Java. If you can memorize them quickly, then it's so much better.

Java Numeric Operators

Most programming languages use the same symbols for their numeric operators. If you already know a modern programming language, then you will notice that the signs for numeric operators of Java are mostly the same with that of the programming language that you are familiar with.

JAVA NUMERIC OPERATORS		
Sign	Operand	Example
+	Addition	8 + 7
-	Subtraction	26 - 9
*	Multiplication	9*5
/	Division	81/3
%	Remainder	23%3

Java Comparison Operators (also known as Relational Operators)

If you are familiar with the comparison operators of other modern programming language, then memorizing the table below would be easy.

JAVA COMPARISON OPERATORS	
less than	<
less than or equal to	<=
greater than	>
greater than or equal to	>=
equal to	==
not equal to	!=

Boolean Logical Operators

The boolean logical operators are different from the comparison operators, be careful when using them.

BOOLEAN LOGICAL OPERATORS	
NOT	!
AND	&&
OR	||
EXCLUSIVE OR	^

The Different Truth Tables

TRUTH TABLE FOR 'NOT'	
A	!A
False	True
True	False

TRUTH TABLE FOR 'AND'		
E1	E2	E1 && E2
False	False	False
False	True	False
True	False	False
True	True	True

*E1 means expression 1 and E2 means expression 2, it's the same with the rest of the tables.

TRUTH TABLE FOR 'OR'		
E1	E2	E1 || E2
False	False	False
False	True	True
True	False	True
True	True	True

TRUTH TABLE FOR 'EXCLUSIVE OR'		
E1	E2	E1 ^ E2
False	False	False
False	True	True
True	False	True
True	True	False

It would be better if you could memorize the different tables right away so you don't need to look whenever you need to confirm something. You will need the tables for the lessons in the succeeding chapters.

Chapter 5: Do the Math and Other Things

It's time to do the Math, the Java way. You can add, subtract, multiply, divide, and get the remainder. It is not difficult to understand, and you will surely appreciate the numerical operators once you started coding your own program. If you still haven't memorized the signs of the different numerical operators in Java, then you can always go back to Chapter 4 to see the table for numerical operators.

Trying your Hands on Java Addition

You can create a program like this:

```
1  public class AdditionProgram {
2     public static void main(String []args) {
3        System.out.println(5 + 9);
4     }
5  }
```

You can also make use of variables like this:

```
1    public class AdditionProgram {

2        public static void main(String []args) {

3
4            int a = 5;
5            int b = 6;
6            System.out.println(a + b);

7
8        }
9    }
```

Trying your Hands on Java Subtraction and other Mathematical Operations

Turn the above example as your guide in creating a simple Java program for subtraction, multiplication, division, and remainder (also called modulo). You can try practicing on your own until you get the hang of it. The more you practice, the more you find it less challenging. You will find it more comfortable to work with Java when that happens.

The Comparison Operators

Comparison operators are also called relational operators. They compare data types, and always give you a boolean value, which is either *true* or *false*. If you are still not familiar with the table, then you can go back and look at it when you start working with relational operators.

A comparison operator goes between two data, known as operands. If you will print this statement:

System.out.println(9<7);

You will get *false* for an answer. A Java program recognizes that it should give a boolen answer when presented with a statement that bears a relational operator.

The equal to (==) and not equal to (!=) operators are also known an equality operators. In Java programming, the programmer can use the equality operators to test the equality of the data. The programmer can test the equality across *int*, *boolean*, or *char* data types. Take the example below:

char sampleChar = 'L';
int sampleNum = 5;
System.out.println(sampleChar==sampleNum);

The above example will print 'false' onscreen because the value in variable sampleChar is not the same as the value that the variable sampleNum holds.

Some Exercises to Try

Now you can test how much you have learned with this simple programming exercise. Don't worry; you will see the correct codes later if you find it a bit challenging. If you see an error message, read the message and try to figure out the mistake that you made. Sometimes, a simply typo error can jeopardize the whole program, unless you spot it immediately. Make sure that you are using your upper cases and lower cases correctly.

1. Declare 'this is my program' as your class; make sure to write it correctly when coding your program.
2. Write a single line comment, anything will do.
3. Assign the value 'false' to the boolean variable isAnything.
4. Assign the value '789' to the int variable isTooMuch.
5. Assign the value of isTooMuch multiplied by 3 to int variable isMuchMuch.
6. Print the value isAnything, isTooMuch, and isMuchMuch.

Try coding the given sample first, on your own, before looking at the answer. You can also try practicing more.

If you are finished, you can look at the answer below. Did you get the same?

```java
1    public class ThisIsMyProgram {

2        // this is my single line comment

3

4        public static void main(String []args) {

5

6        boolean isAnything = false;

7        int isTooMuch = 789;

8        int isMuchMuch = isTooMuch * 3;

9        System.out.println(isAnything);

10       System.out.println(isTooMuch);

11       System.out.println(isMuchMuch);

12

13       }

14   }
```

Now that you know about the Java basics, let's take it a notch higher. You need to be ready for an intro to control flow.

Chapter 6: The Selection Statements

The Java control statements regulate the Java program's order of execution. There are three major categories that you need to understand, and they are:

1. The selection statements if, if-else and switch statements.

2. The loop statements while, do-while and for.

3. The transfer statements break, return, try-catch-finally, continue, and assert.

We use any of the mentioned statements (depending on the needs of the program) if you want to alter the default execution order. For the Java basics, we will discuss about the selection statements and a bit of loop statements.

The Selection Statements

Under this category are: *if* statement, *if-else* statement, and *switch* statement.

Dealing with the *if* Statement

The *if* statement tells the computer to execute a particular block of codes only if the expression within the if statement proves to be true. If the statement is false, then the block of codes will not be executed. The execution will continue for the rest of the codes in the program assuming there are no more selection statements that may prompt the execution due to certain condition.

The if statement follows this syntax:

if (<conditional expression>)

<statement action>

Look at the sample below:

```
1    public class SampleIfStatement {
2
3        public static void main(String[] args) {
4            int a = 20, b = 30;
5            if (a > b)
6                System.out.println("a is greater than b");
7            if (a < b)
8                System.out.println("b is greater than a");
9        }
10 }
```

What do you think will this program print?

Understanding the if-else (or nested if) Statement

Like the *if* statement, the if-else statement also commands the computer to execute a particular block of codes under the if statement only if the expression within the statement is true. If the statement is false, then the else statement must e executed next and only if the condition within the else option is satisfied.

The if statement follows this syntax:

if (<conditional expression>) {

<statement action>

} else {

Take a look at the sample program below:

```
1   public class IfElseStatementDemo {

2

3       public static void main(String[] args) {

4           int a = 20, b = 20;

5           if (a > b) {

6               System.out.println("a is greater than b");

7           } else if (a < b){

8               System.out.println("b is greater than a");

9           } else {

10              System.out.println("a is equal to b");

11          }

12      }

13  }
```

If you will try to analyze it:

Line 4 gives you the given data that the program needs to work with.

Line 5 has a condition that if *a* is greater than b, then it will print "a is greater than b". If you will look at the given data, the statement is false, and that prompts the program to execute the next statement, which is else statement.

Line 7 presented another option or condition; unfortunately, it is still false.

All that's left is to print "*a* is equal to *b*".

The program won't execute the statement under the if or *else-if* statement because both statements are false. However, the else statement at the bottom does not present any condition and that tells the program to print "*a* is equal to *b*", which is actually true.

Try changing the given data in the program and see how the program responds.

The Switch

The switch statement is also known as a case statement where you provide different options for the user and the program will execute it. The switch statement is similar to if-else statement wherein there are option presented and the program will seek the first option that proves to be true. It will execute the statement under the if-else option that returns a value *true*.

The switch statement is more orderly than the if-else statement. It is also easier to maintain the program if it's coded in an orderly fashion. If you have many options to present, then you should use the *switch* statement.

Here is the syntax for the *switch* statement:

```
switch (<non-long integral expression>) {
case 1:

    <statement 1>

    break;


case 2:

    <statement 2>

    break;


case n:

    <statement 2>

    break;


default:

    <statement>
} // end of switch or case statement
```

Look at the sample program below:

```
1    public                    class
     SwitchCaseStatementDemo {

2

3    public static void main(String[]
     args) {

4        int a = 10, b = 30, c = 20;

5        int response = 0;

6        if (a > b && a > c) {

7        response = 1;

8        } else if (b > a && b > c) {

9        response = 2;

10       } else if (c > a && c > b){

11         response = 3;

12       }

13       switch (response) {

14       case 1:

15         System.out.println("a is the biggest
           number");

16         break;

17       case 2:
```

```
18        System.out.println("b is the biggest
          number");

19        break;

20        case 3:

21        System.out.println("c is the biggest
          number");

22        break;

23        default:

24        System.out.println("Error
          encountered, try again");

25        }

26    }

27  }
```

You need to initialize the *int* response, which you need for your *switch* statement. If you remove it, your program will not work.

You can change the data that you need to work with and see the result. You can try changing the condition under each *if-else* statements and see what happens. Make sure that when you change something, the change should be consistent with the whole program. Otherwise, your program won't work or will yield a different result.

The Loop Statements

The loop statements are: *while* statement, *do-while* statement, and *for*.

The ***while*** Statement

The *while* statement tells the program to continue doing the block of codes below it, while the condition or statement remains true. The program will only stop repeating or doing the instructions of the code when the statement becomes false.

This is the syntax for the while loop:

while (<loop condition>) <statements>

Here is the sample program:

```
1    public class SampleWhileLoop {

2

3       public static void main(String[] args)
     {

4                int count = 1;

5                System.out.println("Output
     Numbers 1 - 10");

6                while (count != 11) {

7                        System.out.println(count++
     );

8                }

9        }

10 }
```

We need to initialize *int* count to 1. In Line 6, it only means that when count is already equal to 11, it won't print any more. In Line 7 'count++' tells the program to increment count by 1 so in the next loop it will print 2. It needs to increment count again and in the next loop it will print 3 and so on, and will only stop printing when count equals 11.

The do-while Statement

The *do-while* loop or statement is the similar to the while statement, except the action is given first before the actual condition for the program to check before executing the statement. This can give the program more control because it makes sure that the loop will be performed at least once.

This is the syntax for the do-while statement:

```
do
<loop body>
while (<loop condition>);
```

Here is a sample program:

```
1   public class SampleDoWhileStatement
    {
2
3       public static void main(String[] args)
        {
4           int sheep = 1;
5           System.out.println("Output
            Numbers 1 - 10");
6           do {
7               System.out.println(sheep++);
8           } while (sheep <= 10);
9       }
10  }
```

The for Loop or Statement

The *for* loop is applicable for a task or program that needs to execute a certain block of codes for a certain number of times. It's like repeating the same process repeatedly as long as the condition remains true. You need to initialize the counter that will control the loop.

This is the syntax that you need to follow:

for (<initialization>; <loop condition>; <increment expression>)
<loop body>

Here is the sample program:

```
1  public class SampleForLoop {
2
3      public static void main(String[] args) {
            System.out.println("Output Numbers 1
4          - 10");
            for (int number = 1; number <= 10;
5          number++) {

6                  System.out.println(number);
7          }
8      }
9 }
```

Look at Line 5, you need to initialize your counter 'number', set the condition that number must be less than or equal to 10, and increment number by 1. The next statement prints the counter number, which is initially '1'.

When counter number becomes 2, it is still less than 10, and the counter increments by 1 again. The next statement will now print '2'.

The whole cycle will repeat until the counter number = 10. The counter will still increment by one, and the last statement will print '10'.

Once the counter number turns 11 and it won't satisfy the next condition that the counter number should be less than or equal to 10. The program will no longer execute the remaining statements.

Java is easy and fun to learn. Keep on advancing and discover more wonderful things that you can do with Java programming.

Conclusion

Thank you again for downloading this book!

I hope this book was able to help you to understand the Java basics that you need to know in order to create a Java program with ease.

The next step is to keep on practicing what you have learned and learning more commands as you go along.

Finally, if you enjoyed this book, then I'd like to ask you for a favor, would you be kind enough to leave a review for this book on Amazon? It'd be greatly appreciated!

Please leave a review on Amazon if you enjoyed this book!

Also be sure to signup for my technology and programming newsletter to get your FREE books and learn more about how to program at http://kindlebookspot.com/join-our-tech-community/

Thank you and good luck!

Preview Of 'C# Programming Bootcamp'

This eBook is designed for people who want to know the basics of C#. Basically, it aims to help you master this topic in just 2 weeks. To accomplish that goal, this book contains the important aspects of the C# programming language. It doesn't have unnecessary intros or side stories. This book will teach you what you need to know, so that you will be a proficient C# user after 2 weeks of studying.

C# is an advanced, versatile, and object-oriented language used in computer programming. Microsoft, one of the largest corporations today, developed this programming language as part of its product collection. To prove that C# is useful and reliable, ISO (International Standards Organization) and ECMA (European Computer Manufacturers Association) gave their approval for this computer language.

According to Microsoft, this C# language is designed for CLI (i.e. Common Language Infrastructure). CLI is composed of runtime environments and executable codes that allow the use of advanced programming languages on various computer architectures and platforms.

Here are the main reasons why professional programmers use C#:

- C# is an object-oriented language.
- C# is simple and easy to learn.
- C# is a component-oriented language.
- C# is a structured programming language.
- C# is high-level and versatile.
- C# can produce excellent programs.
- C# allows users to perform compilation using different computer systems.

C#'s Strongest Features

C# has some similarities with older programming languages (i.e. C, C++, and Java). It possesses excellent features that attract millions of programmers worldwide. In this section, let's discuss C#'s best features. Check the list below:

- Indexers
- Assembly Versioning
- Boolean Conditions
- Conditional Compilation
- Windows Integration
- Properties and Events
  - Simple Multithreading

Get the rest of this book on Amazon!

Check Out My Other Books

Below you'll find some of my other popular books that are popular on Amazon and Kindle as well. Simply click on the links below to check them out. Alternatively, you can visit my author page on Amazon to see other work done by me.

Windows 10 Bootcamp

C# Programming Bootcamp

JavaScript Programming Bootcamp

SQL Programming Bootcamp

Wordpress Bootcamp

Python Bootcamp

SEO Bootcamp

3 In 1 Boxset - Windows 10+Wordpress+SEO

5 In 1 Boxset - Python+C#+Java+JavaScript+SQL

If you haven't already, be sure to check out my new website, *KindleBookSpot.com*. This is a new project I've been working on, and I really hope it's valuable to my readers. I made the site because I wanted to give you guys an easier way to find the hottest kindle books at discounted prices, all in one place. Here are some details on what my site has:

- A list of best selling free kindle books
- Discounted fiction and non-fiction books
- A book of the week
- Featured books
- Promote your own book on my site

This site isn't just for readers, it's also a spot where up and coming authors can promote their new books before they turn to best sellers. So if you'd like to promote your own book, check out my site, *KindleBookSpot.com*.

I hope this site will be useful to you, and I hope to see you there!

Subscribe to our growing community at KindleBookSpot to receive notifications when the best books are discounted and free.

Bonus Book 1

Scrum Bootcamp

Learn the Basics of Scrum Programming

More Free and Bargain Books at
KindleBookSpot.com

Table Of Contents

Introduction

I want to thank you and congratulate you for downloading the book, *"Learn the Basics of Scrum Programming in 2 Weeks.*

This book contains proven steps and strategies on how to master the basics of the Scrum framework in a short period of time.

This e-book aims to teach you the core ideas, concepts and techniques used in the Scrum framework. To help you understand "Scrum," this material will explain the basics of "Agile" development and other related techniques.

After reading this book, you will be able to use Scrum in completing your programming tasks. You'll become an effective Scrum practitioner in just 14 days.

Thanks again for downloading this book, I hope you enjoy it!

Chapter 1: Scrum and Agile Development

Scrum is a method used in "Agile" development models. Before discussing what Scrum really is, let's define Agile first. This way, you'll understand how the Scrum method works and how you can use it to complete programming projects.

Agile Development

Basically, Agile is a repetitive and incremental development strategy used in completing projects (e.g. software products). This strategy requires people to work together in order to finish a project quickly. Agile involves a time-boxed repetitive approach, and it requires fast and versatile responses to any changes. According to Agile practitioners, this strategy is a theoretical outline that doesn't indicate any specific activity that a team should do.

Scrum, which is one of the methods used in Agile, defines the techniques and processes that must be done to complete any given project.

Important Note: Agile and its methods (e.g. Scrum) are originally used for software development; thus, Scrum is not a programming language or computing technique. It is a development framework that helps people in completing projects quickly and efficiently. In this book, however, you'll learn how to use Scrum in completing your programming-related projects.

The Major Principles of Agile Development

When using Agile, you should remember the principles listed below:

- Focus on details – Pay close attention to the details of your project. This way, you can attain great project design and technical excellence.

- Less is more – The Agile development framework emphasizes simplicity. Here, you don't have to spice up your projects through insignificant techniques/activities. Solve the problems related to your projects in the simplest way possible.

- Communication is important – To ensure excellent quality, developers (i.e. the people working on the project) must communicate regularly with the business people (the management team or the clients).

- Deliver customer satisfaction – In general, people who use Agile want to satisfy the needs of their customers. These developers use continuous processes to complete the project early and send it to the client/s as soon as possible.

- Changes must be accepted – Agile practitioners must welcome changes (in terms of the working environment and/or project requirements) while working on any project. That means you have to observe all of the changes related to your projects and make the necessary adjustments.

- Trust and motivation – The Agile framework is inherently repetitive and complicated; thus, it requires motivated individuals. Look for people who can be trusted since unreliable staff can ruin your projects.

- Flexibility is the key – Teams must be able to adapt to changing circumstances. You can't be an effective Agile practitioner if you won't adapt to the changes in your working environment.

- The Output is the true measure of success – You can only say that you are successful if you have a working output. Simplicity, productivity, cost-effectiveness and all the "good stuff" are useless if you don't have an output that meets the client's requirements.

Conclusion

Countless companies have benefited from Agile development practices. This is the main reason why Agile frameworks are now adopted in different industries and projects (e.g. programming).

Agile frameworks offer the following benefits:

- Improved delivery time

- Reduced risks and uncertainties

- Better ROI (i.e. Return on Investment) by concentrating on the customers' needs

Chapter 2: The Scrum Framework

What is Scrum?

Software developers define Scrum as a framework for creating and improving complicated products. It is not an approach or methodology for generating new products; instead, it is a development framework that you can use to implement different approaches and methodologies. Scrum can show you the strengths and weaknesses of your development and management strategies, allowing you to improve your overall effectiveness.

This framework involves development groups (called Scrum Teams), events, rules and artifacts. Each of these components plays an important role in the usage and success of the Scrum framework.

The Processes Involved in the Scrum Framework

When using Scrum, you should standardize processes through prescribed events. Each event is time-boxed, which means it has a specific deadline. You'll learn more about "events" in a later chapter.

Sprint

Sprint, a time-box usually measured in weeks, serves as the core of Scrum. Basically, Sprint is a period of time in which an increment of a product is generated. A new Sprint begins as soon as the previous one gets completed. Sprints have the following elements:

- Sprint Planning – The people involved in the project will decide on the tasks that must be accomplished within the Sprint. Each member of the Scrum Team must participate in this collaborative activity.

- Daily Meetings – Scrum Teams need to create plans and share updates on a daily basis. To achieve this, each team must have a 15-minute meeting each day.

- Sprint Review – This event occurs at the conclusion of a Sprint. Here, the members of the Scrum Team review the product increment and update the records of the project, if necessary.

- Sprint Retrospective – It happens just before the planning phase of the next Sprint. In this event, the members of the Scrum Team check their performance and look for ways to improve. This allows them to attain better results during the next Sprint.

The Members of a Scrum Team

Scrum Teams involve three main roles, which are:

1. The "ScrumMaster" (also written as "Scrum Master") – This person acts as the leader of the team. The ScrumMaster needs to:

- Make sure that the Scrum framework and the resulting processes run efficiently.

- Identify and remove obstacles that affect the team's productivity.

- Organize and facilitate important meetings.

2. The Product Owner – This person maximizes the team's efficiency and the product's value. In general, the product owner needs to manage the backlog of the project. Project backlog management involves the following:

- Clear expression of items within the project backlog

- Effective arrangement of project backlog items to attain the team's objectives

- Maximize the overall value of the team's performance

- Make sure that the project backlog is clear, transparent and accessible to all team members. Additionally, the backlog must inform the members about what needs to be done or improved.

- Make sure that each member understands the project backlog items.

  - A product owner may perform the tasks listed above, or ask the team members to do so. In any case, the product owner is solely accountable for those tasks.

  - A product owner is just one person, not a group of people. This person may express the needs/wants of other people in the project's backlog. However, each item present in the backlog must be listed under the product owner's name.

  - The whole team must respect the product owner's decisions. The team members should check the project backlog to know more about the decisions of the product owner.

  3. The Team – This term refers to the members of a team other than the ScrumMaster and product owner. In general, the "Team" aspect of a Scrum team must be able to organize itself and perform different functions. This aspect is composed of testers, analysts, developers and designers.

Other members (e.g. engineers and architects) may be added to a team, depending on the project involved.

For a "team" to be effective, it should be large enough to finish the tasks and small enough to stay versatile. The ideal size of a "team" is five to nine members (excluding the ScrumMaster and Product Owner). If the members are less than five, the manpower may not be sufficient to complete the project within the assigned Sprint. However, if the members are more than nine, the team will need excessive coordination.

Conclusion

Scrum is an Agile framework that specifies roles, rules and tasks to ensure consistency. You can use it for any project or organization, provided that you will follow all the rules of Scrum development.

Chapter 3: Events

Agile practitioners consider Scrum as a set of events and their resulting "artifacts." As mentioned earlier, Scrum uses time-boxed events to manage projects. The term "time-boxed" means that each event has a predetermined deadline. This allows the members of the Scrum Team to see their overall progress in completing the project. The most important Scrum events are:

Sprint

In this event, the Scrum Team develops a working increment of the product. Usually, a Sprint involves 1 month or 2 weeks, and this time period is applied on all of the Sprints in a project. Consistency in terms of the time period is important. It would be confusing and inefficient if the team members need to adjust to varying deadlines.

The Goal of a Sprint

Each sprint has a specific goal. The goal informs team members regarding the increment's purpose. The team sets this goal during the planning phase of the sprint. The product owner and the rest of the team set and clarify the sprint's scope. They also make adjustments on the sprint whenever they discover new things regarding the project.

Sprint Planning

This stage allows you to set the activities that you must complete within the sprint. The planning stage usually lasts for four hours for two-week sprints and eight hours for month-long sprints. The ScrumMaster is responsible in ensuring that meetings take place and that the needed members are present. Also, the ScrumMaster must facilitate the meeting to ensure the productivity and timeliness of the discussion.

In general, sprint planning concentrates on the following questions:

- What should be completed in the current increment?

- What can be completed in the current increment?

- How can the entire team achieve the goals of the sprint?

This stage needs the following inputs:

- The project backlog

- The latest increment of the project

- The estimated capacity of the scrum team

- The previous performance of the scrum team

The entire team will discuss the features/functionalities that must be developed within the current sprint. The product owner should clarify the most important parts of the sprint through the project backlog. The team members choose the items that will be included in the backlog, since they know what they can accomplish within the time-box assigned to them. The tasks are completed collaboratively, an approach that minimizes rework.

After deciding on the feature/s to be developed, the team must decide on how to add those features into the project. The backlog items chosen for the sprint as well as the strategy for implementing them are known as sprint backlog.

The tasks to be completed within a sprint are approximated in the planning stage. They may be of different sizes and complexities. Once the sprint planning has been completed, the project is separated into tasks that last up to a whole day. This approach helps ScrumMasters in assigning tasks and checking the progress of the project. If the members of the scrum team realize that they have too little (or too much) tasks, they may talk to the ScrumMaster and the product owner to make the necessary changes.

The members may also ask others (i.e. people who aren't part of the current Scrum Team) to help in the planning stage. Non-members can provide cost estimates, technical suggestions or practical tips.

Daily Meetings

These meetings last for 15 minutes. They are held daily to understand the things that have been completed in the previous day and formulate a plan for the current day. Some Scrum practitioners refer to these meetings as "Stand Up" meetings.

Daily meetings are conducted at the same place and time. This way, the team members can reduce the complexity of the meetings and focus on what they should do.

During a meeting, each member of the Scrum team must answer the following questions:

- How did he/she help the Scrum team in meeting the goal?

- How can he/she assist the team in meeting the sprint goal?

- Did he/she notice any obstacle that stops him/her or the whole Scrum team from attaining the sprint's goal?

Some people think that daily meetings are held to track the project's progress. However, this is a faulty assumption. Actually, daily meetings are conducted to plan what must be done for the project, not just to check what has been accomplished.

According to Scrum experts, all of the team members are responsible for the productivity and effectiveness of the Daily Meetings. That means each member must help in conducting the daily meetings, although the ScrumMaster performs the managerial tasks involved.

Here are the benefits offered by daily meetings:

- These meetings improve the communication between team members.

- Daily meetings help in identifying project-related problems. They also help in solving problems quickly and efficiently.

- They promote and emphasize fast decision-making.

- They improve the project-related knowledge of the team members.

Sprint Review

The Scrum Team should hold this event before concluding each sprint. In this stage, the team members should review the project increment before releasing it (i.e. either to the client or to the next sprint session). During a sprint review, all of the stakeholders (i.e. the people affected by or involved in the project) should check what was accomplished in the current sprint. These stakeholders will give their suggestions as to what must be accomplished in the next sprint session. They will base these suggestions on two factors:

- Their findings from the Sprint review
- The changes that were made to the project backlog during the current sprint

The goal of this stage is to get feedback from the stakeholders and ensure consistent progress.

In general, the duration of a sprint review depends on the sprint's time-box. Sprint reviews for 2-week sprints last for two hours. Month-long sprints, on the other hand, require 4-hour reviews; thus, each week spent on a sprint requires one hour of review.

During a Sprint Review, the ScrumMaster should:

- Make sure that the meeting occurs.

- Inform the team members regarding the goal/purpose of the sprint review.

- Help the members to focus on the important topics.

- Make sure that the meeting ends in a timely manner.

The following events occur during a sprint review:

- The product owner invites non-members to attend the review (optional).

- The product owner discusses the project backlog. He/she will inform everyone regarding the backlog items that have been completed. Then, he/she will enumerate the backlog items that were not finished within the sprint.

- The team members discuss the positive aspects of the sprint, the problems they encountered and how they solved those problems.

- The team members demonstrate the work that they have completed. They will also answer questions, if any, regarding the project increment.

- The whole group (i.e. both members and non-members) decides on what should be done in the next sprint; thus, the review stage generates important inputs that are useful for the next sprint session.

- The members of the Scrum team check the aspects (e.g. budget, timeline, marketplace, capabilities, potential, etc.) related to the release of a product increment.

- Once the sprint review has been completed, the Scrum team will update the project backlog. These updates define the backlog items that will be used for the subsequent sprint.

Sprint Retrospective

This stage happens before the start of the next sprint's planning stage. The sprint retrospective of 2-week sprints lasts for one hour while that of month-long sprints lasts for three hours.

Basically, a sprint retrospective aims to:

- Utilize the information gathered from the previous sprint session in terms of tools, people, processes and relationships.

- Determine the backlog items that worked well.

- Identify the sprint's areas of improvement.

- Create a plan   for improving the project's effectiveness and overall quality.

Scrum allows you to review your previous performance; thus, it helps you to improve the effectiveness of your subsequent sprint sessions.

Chapter 4: Artifacts

In Scrum, "artifacts" give important data to the stakeholders and team members; thus, artifacts allow you to understand the current project, the tasks that has been completed and the processes involved in the project. The Scrum framework involves the following artifacts:

- Project backlog
- Sprint backlog
- Increment
- Burn-Down chart

The list given above shows the mandatory artifacts of the Scrum framework. In some situations, Scrum teams require other types of artifacts.

Let's discuss the four mandatory artifacts in detail:

The Project Backlog

Basically, this artifact is a set of features/characteristics that the Scrum team must add to the product. It provides the team with information that they can use to improve the project increment.

The project backlog specifies the functions, features, repairs, enhancements and requirements that the project requires. The items within this backlog have the following attributes:

- Value
- Order
- Description
- Estimate

Scrum practitioners use the term "user story" when referring to any of the attributes given above. In general, the product owner must take care of all aspects (e.g. content, ordering, availability, etc.) related to the project backlog.

This artifact evolves as the project progresses. The initial version may hold only the most basic requirements. As the Scrum team gets more information about the project, the project backlog will be developed further. The product owner must update this artifact regularly to retain its effectiveness. Basically, the project backlog will exist as long as the product related to it exists.

As the team works on the product, the project backlog turns into a bigger and more detailed list. Moreover, the changes in technology, market conditions, or business needs may affect the project backlog. This is the reason why many people consider this backlog as a "live" output.

The refinement of the project backlog involves the addition of details, approximations and priority orders to the items within the artifact. It is a continuous process that the product owner performs. The entire team decides on when and how the refinement is done.

Important Note: The product owner may update the project backlog anytime, depending on his/her situation.

Often, high-priority backlog items are clearer and more defined than lower-priority ones. Clear and precise details allow team members to make correct estimates.

This artifact allows team members to refine requirements so they can use it for the upcoming sprint. The backlog items that the Scrum team can develop are considered to be ready for usage in the next sprint's planning stage.

The Sprint Backlog

This artifact is the combination of project backlog items chosen for the sprint, and a strategy to create the increment and attain the sprint's goal.

This kind of backlog specifies the functionalities that can be added to the next project increment. It also defines the tasks and activities needed to add those functionalities to the product.

As new tasks are required, the members of the team update the sprint backlog. The team members will also update the remaining tasks on a regular basis. Obviously, it's important to inform the whole team whenever a task gets added or completed. The team should also remove unnecessary items from this backlog.

Keep in mind that only members of the team can modify the sprint backlog. Additionally, this artifact must be visible and accessible to all of the team members.

Increment

The term "increment" refers to the project backlog items that the team has completed. When concluding a sprint, the increment should be a usable product. The product should be usable, even if the product owner doesn't want to release it yet.

The entire team should agree on what will be considered as increments. This differs significantly for each Scrum team. However, each member must understand clearly what "increment" means for the team. This allows members to determine the progress or completion of the project.

The knowledge about increments also allows members to identify the backlog items that must be selected. The objective of every sprint session is to create increments of usable products.

In general, each Scrum team should complete a product increment within a sprint. Since increments are usable products, the product owner may release it to the market as is.

Some Scrum teams consider increment knowledge as a requirement. That means increment knowledge is involved in the organization's standards, guidelines or conventions. If increment knowledge is not mandatory, the ScrumMaster must define the increments appropriate for the project.

The Burn-Down Chart

During a sprint session, the team members may sum up the remaining tasks inside the project backlog. The Scrum team measures the remaining tasks during each daily meeting. This approach allows teams to determine their chances of achieving their goal/s and manage their progress.

The Burn-Down chart is a technique for tracking the activities completed by the team. Agile practitioners have used this technique in measuring and managing their team's progress.

Product owners track the remaining tasks during each sprint review. Then, he/she compares these tasks with those from previous sprints. This approach helps product owners to assess the team's progress toward completing the assigned tasks.

Important Note: The product owner must share this artifact will each stakeholder.

Conclusion

Scrum involves different outputs that are known as artifacts. You must generate and use these artifacts while implementing the Scrum framework. By doing so, you can increase your chances of meeting your project goals.

Chapter 5: The User Stories

In the "software development" industry, product features serve important roles. These features attract consumers and encourage them to purchase or use the completed product. In general terminology, product features are called "requirements." The success of a software generation project depends on knowing the users' needs precisely and incorporating them into the finished product. That means that the team members should know the requirements or product features that they need to work on before starting any project.

Kent Beck, an American software engineer, coined the term "User Stories" back in 1999. A user story, which is narrated from the user's point of view, informs software developers regarding the needs of the end-user instead of what the product can do for him/her. The development perspective changed from being "product-focused" to "user-focused." Because of their effectiveness, user stories became standard requirements for teams that use any "Agile" framework.

When it comes to the Scrum framework, project backlogs serve as a collection of user stories. The ScrumMaster must identify, prioritize and discuss these user stories during the sprint planning stage.

In most cases, Scrum teams base their estimations and goals on the user stories of the project.

The Structure of a User Story

User Stories follow this format:

As a <kind of user>,

I need to <complete a task>,

So I can <attain a goal/enjoy a benefit/receive something.>

Let's analyze how user stories are formed. Here, let's assume that a bank client wants to withdraw money from an ATM.

User Story – Client's ATM Withdrawal

As a Client, I need to withdraw money from an ATM, so I can get the cash I need without going inside the bank.

The Acceptance Criteria

User stories involve acceptance criteria (i.e. tests that gauge the effectiveness of a user story). The acceptance criteria helps Scrum teams in analyzing the effects of the user story/stories on the current project.

Here's a simple acceptance criteria for the user story given above:

First Acceptance Criterion:

Given Information:

The client is creditworthy.

The debit/credit card is acceptable.

The machine has enough cash.

Situation:

The client needs the money.

Then:

Make sure that the proper account is charged.

Make sure that the machine dispenses the right amount.

Make sure that the machine returns the client's debit/credit card.

Second Acceptance Criterion:

Given Information:

The client's account doesn't have enough funds.

The client's card is acceptable.

Situation:

The client needs the money

Then:

Display a rejection message on the screen.

Make sure that machine doesn't dispense any money.

Make sure that the machine returns the card.

How to Write a User Story

Since the project backlog holds the user stories, the product owner is responsible for managing the project's user stories. However, the product owner isn't the only person who can write a user story. Basically, any team member can accomplish this task. That means the ScrumMaster may spread this responsibility across the entire team.

The Non-Functional Requirements in a User Story

Scrum teams may incorporate non-functional requirements into a user story. In the example given above, the non-functional requirement is the ATM's 24/7 availability.

How to Manage a User Story

You should use the project backlog in order to manage a user story. Often, Scrum teams arrange user stories based on their importance. The most important stories are improved to the fullest, while non-important ones are worked on minimally. For each sprint, the product owner records the most important (and the most detailed) user stories in the sprint backlog. When adding a user story to any backlog, the product owner checks its priority: he/she will place the user story in the project backlog according to its priority.

Important Note: Team members can remove or reprioritize user stories, depending on their situation.

The Benefits Offered by User Stories

User stories help development groups to focus on the end-users. This is important since ultimately, the end-users will buy and use the product once it is released in the market. Thus, user stories help Scrum teams to connect with their end-users.

The structure of user stories helps Scrum teams to determine the goals/values/benefits that the end-users want to achieve.

The acceptance criteria, which is an important aspect of any user story, can help Scrum teams in analyzing their projects objectively.

The members of a Scrum team may modify user stories while working on a project. For instance, they may split a user story into smaller ones if its scope grows too large. The team members may also change the acceptance criteria used for the project.

Since the Scrum team delivers the product increment to the client each time a sprint ends. They may acquire feedback and suggestions that can be used in the subsequent sprints.

Conclusion

User stories bring you closer to the end-users of your projects; thus, these stories can help you generate usable products and prevent undesirable results.

Chapter 6: Estimation

The Scrum team should make their estimations during the planning stage. The purpose of these estimations is to analyze the user stories based on priority and the team's capability. The product owner makes sure that the top-priority user stories are understandable, can be used for estimations, and are included in the project backlog.

Since the whole team is responsible for completing and delivering the project increment, extreme care should be taken when choosing user stories. The members of the team need to base their decisions on the increment's target size and the overall effort needed in the project.

Important Note: The increment's size is measured through story points. After determining the increment size, the team should estimate the effort needed using the data from previous sprints.

The Techniques Used in Estimation

When making estimates, focus on each user story's degree of complexity/difficulty. Here are the scales that you can use in assessing the difficulty or complexity of user stories:

The Numeric Sizing – This is a scale that ranges from 1 to 10.

Shirt Sizes – (S, XS, M, L, XL, etc.)

The Fibonacci Sequence – In this scale, you will add a number to the one that precedes it. The sum will be used as the next number.

The Poker Estimation Approach

In this approach, you will derive estimates by playing a poker-like card game. The whole team can help in implementing this approach. With Poker Estimation, you can generate reliable estimates without spending too much time or effort.

This approach requires multiple decks of playing cards. Using the numbers printed on the cards, follow the Fibonacci sequence. The cards' numbers represent story points (i.e. the value used in measuring user stories).

Each member should have a deck of cards. You have to assign a moderator – this person will read the descriptions/explanations for the User Story. The product owner will answer any question brought up during the session.

The team members (also called "estimators") should express their estimate by selecting a card privately. The estimators should keep their card hidden until all of them have chosen a card. Once everyone has selected a card, they should reveal their estimates simultaneously.

It's possible that the estimations will vary significantly during the initial round. Each estimator should explain their estimates. Make sure that no personal questions are asked – the team members should focus on explaining their opinions/decisions.

While the users explain their opinions, the moderator should take notes. These notes can help the team in developing the user stories. Once a round is completed, each member should make another estimate. They will hide their card/s until all of them have made a selection. Then, they will reveal their cards at the same time.

Repeat this procedure until you get a single estimation. Keep in mind that the rounds required for estimation may vary, depending on the user stories you are working on.

The Methods Used in the Poker Estimation Approach

Analogy – This method requires you to compare user stories. Basically, you should compare the current user story with the ones you have implemented. Since this method is based on actual data, it generates accurate results.

Disaggregation – In this estimation method, you'll split a user story into smaller ones. The user stories used in sprints normally last for three to six days; thus, if you encounter a User Story that lasts for seven days or more, you have to divide it into smaller, more manageable portions. As a bonus, this method helps you to make sure that you have comparable user methods.

Expert Opinion – This method requires the feedback/suggestions of an industry expert. Since each team member is closely involved in the Scrum project, they have sufficient knowledge and experience regarding the subject matter; thus, they can be considered as "experts."

Here, the experts will base their opinions/estimates on their experience and knowledge, not on their intuition.

Conclusion

The poker approach is a fun and productive method that you can use to generate Scrum estimates. Since it allows people to share and discuss their opinions, the team will gain more information regarding the current user story.

Conclusion

Thank you again for downloading this book!

I hope this book was able to help you master the basics of Scrum in just two weeks.

The next step is to use this development framework in completing your computer programs.

Finally, if you enjoyed this book, then I'd like to ask you for a favor, would you be kind enough to leave a review for this book on Amazon? It'd be greatly appreciated!

Please leave a review on Amazon if you enjoyed this book!

Also be sure to signup for my technology and programming newsletter to get your FREE books and learn more about how to program at kindlebookspot.com/join-our-tech-community/.

Thank you and good luck!

Bonus Book 2
Hacking Bootcamp

Learn the Basics of Computer Hacking

More discounted books at
<u>kindlebookspot.com</u>

Table Of Content

Introduction

I want to thank you and congratulate you for downloading the book, *"Learn the Basics of Computer Hacking (Security, Penetration Testing, How to Hack).*

This book contains proven steps and strategies on how to hack computer networks.

This e-book will teach you the basic ideas and concepts related to hacking. It will explain the tools, methods and techniques used by experienced hackers. By reading this material, you can conduct reconnaissance and software attacks against your target networks.

Thanks again for downloading this book, I hope you enjoy it!

Chapter 1: Hacking — General Information

This book can help you become a great computer hacker. With this material, you will be able to:

Think like a hacker — Since you'll know the methods and techniques used in hacking, you can attack networks or protect yourself from other people.

Learn about "ethical hacking" — You don't have to use your skills to infiltrate networks or steal data. In the world of IT (i.e. information technology), you may use your new skills to help businesses and organizations in preventing hacking attacks; thus, you can earn money by being a "good" hacker.

Impress your friends and family members — You may show off your hacking abilities to other people. This way, you can establish your reputation as a skilled programmer or computer-user.

Hackers — Who are they?

Hackers are people who love to play with computer networks or electronic systems. They love to discover how computers work. According to computer experts, hackers are divided into two main types:

White Hat Hackers – These people are known as "good hackers." A white hat hacker uses his/her skills for legal purposes. Often, he/she becomes a security expert who protects companies and organizations from the black hat hackers (see below).

Black Hat Hackers – This category involves hackers who use their skills for malicious/illegal purposes. These hackers attack networks, vandalize websites and steal confidential information.

Important Note: These terms originated from Western movies where protagonists wore white hats and villains wore black hats.

The Hierarchy of Computer Hackers

In this part of the book, hackers are categorized according to their skill level. Study this material carefully since it can help you measure your progress.

The Would-Be Hackers – In this category, you'll find beginners who don't really know what they are doing. These hackers normally have poor computer skills. They use the programs and hacking tools created by others without knowing how things work.

The Intermediate Hackers – These hackers are familiar with computers, operating systems and programming languages. Normally, an intermediate hacker knows how computer scripts work. However, just like a would-be hacker, an intermediate hacker doesn't create his or her own tools.

The Elite Hackers – This category is composed of experienced hackers. In general, an elite hacker creates tools and programs that are useful in attacking or defending computer networks. Also, an elite hacker can access a system without getting caught. All hackers want to attain this level.

The Requirements

You can't become an elite hacker overnight. To get the necessary skills, you have to be patient and tenacious. Focus on the things you have to do (e.g. write your own programs, practice your hacking skills, read more books, etc.). By spending your time and effort on things that can turn you into a great hacker, you can reach the "elite" level quickly.

Hacking experts claim that creativity is important, especially for beginners. With creativity, you can easily find multiple solutions to a single problem. You won't have to worry about limited resources or options. If you are creative enough, you will surely find excellent answers for difficult problems.

You should also have the desire to learn more. Hacking involves complex processes that evolve as years go by. You should be willing to spend hours, days, or even weeks studying network structures and attack strategies. If you don't have the time or patience for this kind of detailed work, you have minimal chances of becoming an expert hacker.

Chapter 2: Programming Skills

To become an effective hacker, you should have sufficient skills in programming. The ability to create and manipulate computer programs can go a long way. This ability can help you cover your tracks or confuse security experts. However, if you want to be an ethical hacker, you may use your skills to create defensive computer programs.

Well, it is true that you can purchase ready-to-use programs and hacking tools online. That means you may execute hacking attacks or defend your network without programming anything. However, relying on programs created by others won't help you become a great hacker. Anybody can purchase and use a hacking program – it takes skill and knowledge to create one.

Whenever you attack, defend or test a network, you should understand everything that is related to the activity. Since hacking attacks and system tests involve programs, programming skills can help you attain effectiveness and accuracy in completing your tasks.

If you know how to program, then you'll enjoy the following benefits:

- Other hackers will consider you as an expert.

- You can create programs specifically for your needs. For instance, if you need to stop a certain virus, you can create your own security program to accomplish your goal. You won't have to go online and try various antivirus programs that are often expensive.

- You will have more confidence in your skills. Just like any other endeavor, hacking will be way much easier and simpler if the person trusts his or her skills.

- Simply put, don't rely on hacking programs available in the market. Study some programming languages and acquire the necessary skills. By doing so, you will gain access to a new world of computing and hacking.

How to Start your Programming Journey?

It would be great if you'll study HTML first. HTML (i.e. hypertext markup language) is a programming language that forms all of the websites you see online. If you are planning to attack or establish a website, you have to know how to use the HTML language. Most people say that HTML is simple and easy to master. That means you can learn this language easily even if you have never programmed anything before.

After mastering HTML, you should learn the C programming language. C is the most popular computer language today. It forms most of the tools that hackers use. It can help you create your own viruses or defensive programs.

A Study Plan

Here's a study plan that can help you master any programming language:

- Buy a "beginner's book" about your chosen language. Before making a purchase, read the reviews made by book owners. This way, you won't have to waste your time and/or money on a useless material.

- Once you have learned how to use the language, you must practice it regularly.

- Almost all programming books contain exercises and practice problems. Work on these exercises and problems to hone your skills further.

- If you encounter anything difficult, don't skip or ignore it. Try to understand how that "thing" works and how it is related to programming and/or hacking. You won't learn many things if you'll skip complex ideas.

- Look for an online forum for programmers. Most of the time, experienced programmers are willing to help beginners. That means you can just go online and ask the "pros" whenever you encounter problems in your studies.

- Apply what you learn. It would be great if you'll use the language to create your own computer programs.

Chapter 3: Passwords

These days, passwords serve as the exclusive form of protection for networks and websites. If you have this piece of information, you will gain complete access to the owner's account. This is the reason why hackers use different tools and techniques just to get passwords.

Password Cracking – Traditional Approaches

The following list shows you the traditional techniques used in cracking passwords:

Guessing – This approach is only effective for weak passwords. For example, if the user created his password based on personal information (e.g. phone number, date of birth, favorite animal, etc.), you can easily determine the password by trying out different possibilities. This technique becomes more effective if the hacker knows a few things about the user.

Shoulder Surfing – Here, you will look over the target's shoulder as he or she types the password. This approach can give you excellent results if the target is a slow typist.

Social Engineering – In this technique, you'll exploit the target's trust in order to get the needed information. For instance, you may call the target and pretend that you belong to the company's IT department. You can tell the target that you need his password so you can access his account and make some important updates.

Password Cracking – Modern Techniques

In this section, you'll learn about the latest techniques used in cracking passwords.

Important Note: This section uses some computer programs that you need to install.

The Dictionary Attack

In this approach, you have to use a text file that contains common passwords. You will try each password to see which one works. This approach offers ease and simplicity. However, you can only use it for weak passwords. To help you understand this technique, let's analyze the following example:

A hacker uses Brutus (i.e. a popular password-cracking program) to access an FTP (i.e. file transfer protocol) server.

Before discussing the example, let's talk about FTP servers first. An FTP server allows you to send or receive files through the internet. If a hacker gains access to a site's FTP server, he may manipulate or remove the files within that server.

Now, you're ready for the example. Here we go:

The hacker visits the FTP server's login page.

Then, he launches Brutus to crack the server's password.

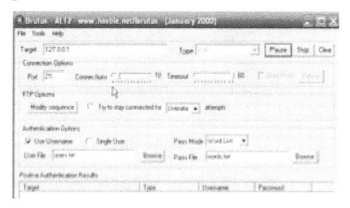

He indicates the server's type (i.e. FTP) and IP address.

He enters a valid username.

He chooses the text file that contains the password list.

He clicks on the Start button. The Brutus program will connect to the FTP server and try to log in using the passwords inside the text file. If the process is successful, Brutus will show the correct password in its "Positive Authentication Results" section. Here's a screenshot:

Important Note: Elite hackers use a proxy whenever they use this kind of computer program. Basically, a proxy hides your IP address by transmitting connection requests from a different computer. This is important since multiple login attempts create a lot of electronic "footprints."

The Brute-Force Approach

IT experts claim that this approach can crack any type of password. Here, the hacker tries all possible combinations of numbers, letters and special symbols until he gets into the targeted account. The main drawback of this approach is that it is time-consuming. This is understandable – you have to try thousands of possible passwords just to access the target's account.

The speed of this approach depends on two factors:

- The password's complexity
- The computer's processing power

Brutus, the hacking tool used in the previous example, can also launch brute-force attacks against a server. Here's how it works:

Specify the target's IP address and server type. In the "Pass Mode" section, select "Brute Force" and hit "Range." The image below will serve as your guide:

The screen will show you a dialog box (see below). Use this dialog box to configure the brute-force approach. Obviously, your job will be way much simpler if you have some idea about the target's password. For instance, if you know that the website requires passwords with 5-10 characters, you'll be able to narrow down the possibilities and shorten the whole process.

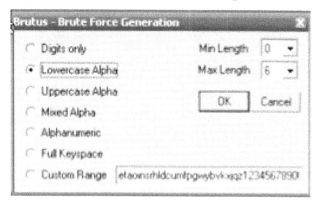

Hit the OK button. Brutus will log in to the targeted server by trying all possible passwords. You'll see the results on the program's GUI (i.e. graphical user interface).

Phishing

In this technique, you'll steal confidential information (e.g. passwords) by fooling the victim. For example, a hacker pretended to be a bank representative and sent an email to the target user. The email required the user to change her password by clicking on a link. When the user clicked on the link, she saw a website similar to that of the actual bank. The website, however, is just a replica. Any information entered there will go to the hacker's database or email account.

Important Note: Elite hackers use HTML to create phishing sites that look like official ones.

Here are the things you need to do when creating a phishing website:

Choose your target – Most hackers mimic the websites of email service providers. There are two reasons for this:

Users log in to their email account regularly. That means the hacker has a lot of opportunities to fool his target.

Email accounts are extremely useful. Most of the time, an email account is linked to other accounts (e.g. bank accounts). Thus, you can get loads of information about the user just by hacking his email account.

> For this book, let's assume that you want to create a phishing site for Gmail.

Copy the official webpage – Launch Mozilla Firefox (hackers recommend this browser because it is secure and customizable) and access the login page of the actual website. Press CTRL+S on your keyboard to create a local copy of the webpage.

Rename the file – After saving the webpage, change its name to "index.htm." The index page is the first webpage that shows up whenever someone reaches a website; thus, you want the target user to believe that he reached the index webpage of the real site.

Create a script – You should create a computer script that will record the user's login information. Most hackers use the PHP scripting language to accomplish this task. The image below shows you a basic PHP script that records login credentials.

Launch Notepad and enter the script. Save the file as "phish.php".

```php
<?php

Header("Location:
https://www.google.com/accounts/ServiceLogin?service=mail&passive=
true&rm=false&continue=http%3A%2F%2Fmail.google.com%2Fmail%2F
%3Fui%3Dhtml%26zy%3Dl&bsv=1k96igf4806cy&ltmpl=default&ltmplcac
he=2 ");

$handle = fopen("list.txt", "a");

Foreach($_GET as $variable => $value) {
  fwrite($handle, $variable);
  fwrite($handle, "=");
  fwrite($handle, $value);
  fwrite($handle, "\r\n");
}

Fwrite($handle, "\r\n");
fclose($handle);

exit;
?>
```

Create an empty .txt file and save it as "list.txt".

Add the script to the webpage – Use the file named index.htm using Notepad. Press CTRL+F, type "action", and click on "Find Next". Here's a screenshot:

Look for "action" in the script's "form id" section. You'll see a URL there – delete it and type "phish.php". By doing so, you're instructing the form to send the user's information to your PHP script rather than to Google.

Search for the part that says method="post". Replace "post" with "get" so that the code snippet is method="get".

Save the file and close it.

Upload the HTML file to a website host – The hosting service provider will give you a URL for the rigged webpage. You may use that URL for hacking purposes.

If you'll visit the webpage, you'll see that it looks exactly like the official Gmail login page. That webpage will record the usernames and passwords that will be entered into it. It will save the information side the empty .txt file.

Rainbow Tables

Basically, rainbow tables are huge lists of hash values for each possible character combination. To get a hash value, you have to transform a password (or a character combination) by running it through an algorithm. This is a one-way type of encryption: you cannot use the hash value to determine the original data. Most website databases use MD5, a mathematical algorithm used for hashing, to protect passwords.

Let's assume that you registered for a site. You entered your desired login credentials (i.e. username and password). Once you hit the "Submit" button, the algorithm will process the password and store the hash value into the site's database.

Since it's impossible to determine passwords using hash values, you may be wondering how networks know whether your password is right or wrong. Well, when you enter your login credentials, the system runs those pieces of information through the algorithm. Then, it will compare the resulting hash with those saved in the site's database. If the hash values match, you will be logged in.

Mathematical algorithms such as MD5 produce complex strings out of simple passwords. For instance, if you'll encrypt "cheese" using MD5, you'll get: fea0f1f6fede90bd0a925b4194deac11.

According to expert hackers, this method is more effective than the brute-force approach. Once you have created rainbow tables (i.e. lists of hash values), you can crack passwords quickly.

How to Prevent these Password-Cracking Techniques?

Social Engineering

To stop "social engineers," you must be careful and attentive. If someone calls you, and you think that he's using social engineering tactics on you, ask him questions that can prove his identity.

Important Note: Some elite hackers research about their targets. That means they may "prove their identity" by answering your questions. Because of this, if you still doubt what the person says, you should talk to the head of whichever department he says he's from to get more information.

Shoulder Surfing

While entering your login credentials, make sure that no one sees what you are typing. If you see someone suspicious, approach him and practice your wrestling skills. Well, not really. You just have to be careful in entering your information.

Guessing

To prevent this attack, don't use a password that is related to your personal information. Regardless of the love you have for your pet or spouse, you should never use their name as your password.

Dictionary Attack

You can protect yourself from this attack easily – don't use passwords that are found in the dictionary. No, replacing letters with numbers (e.g. banana – b4n4n4) isn't safe. It would be best if you'll combine letters, numbers and special characters when creating a password.

Brute-Force Approach

To prevent this technique, you should use a long password that involves lots of numbers and special symbols. Long and complicated passwords pose difficult problems for "brute-forcers." If the hacker cannot crack your password after several days of trying, he will probably look for another target.

Phishing

To protect yourself against this technique, you just have to check your browser's address bar. For instance, if you should be in www.facebook.com but the address bar shows a different URL (e.g. www.pacebook.com, www.faccbook.com, www.focebook.com, etc.), you'll know that a hacker is trying to fool you.

Rainbow Tables

You can prevent this technique by creating a long password. According to elite hackers, generating hash tables for long passwords involves lots of resources.

"Password Crackers"

Here are the programs used by hackers in cracking passwords:

SolarWinds

Can and Abel

RainbowCrack

THC Hydra

John the Ripper

Chapter 4: How to Hack a Network

In this chapter, you will learn how to hack websites and computer networks. Study this material carefully because it will teach you important ideas and techniques related to hacking.

Footprinting

The term "footprinting" refers to the process of collecting data about a computer network and the company or organization it is linked to. This process serves as the initial step of most hacking attacks. Footprinting is necessary since a hacker must know everything about his target before conducting any attack.

Here are the steps that you need to take when footprinting a website:

You should research about the names and email addresses used in the website. This data can be extremely useful if you're planning to execute social engineering tactics against the target.

Get the website's IP address. To get this information, visit this site and enter the target's URL. Then, hit the "Get IP" button. The screen will show you the IP address of your target website after a few seconds.

Ping the target's server to check if it is currently active. Obviously, you don't want to waste your time attacking a "dead" target. Elite hackers use www.just-ping.com to accomplish this task. Basically, www.just-ping.com pings any website from various parts of the globe.

To use this tool, just enter the target's URL or IP address into the textbox and hit "ping!" Here's a screenshot:

The webpage will show you whether the target is active or not.

Perform a WHOIS search on the website. Visit http://whois.domaintools.com and enter the target's URL. The screen will show you lots of data about the person/company/organization that owns the target website.

Important Note: A WHOIS search provides hackers with different types of information such as names, addresses and phone numbers. This search also gives website-specific details (e.g. the website's DNS, the domain's expiration date, etc.).

Port Scanning

This is the second phase of the hacking process. After collecting information about the target, you should perform a "port scan." Basically, a "port scan" is a process that detects the open ports and listening devices present in a network. That means you can use this step to identify the target's weaknesses and defense systems.

The following exercise will illustrate how port scanning works:

Download Nmap from this site: http://nmap.org/download.html. Then, install the program into your computer.

Note: This software works for Windows and Macintosh computers.

Launch Nmap and enter the target's URL. For this exercise, let's assume that you want to hack a site called www.target-site.com.

Look for the "Profile" section and click on its dropdown button. The screen will show you several scanning options. Most of the time, elite hackers perform quick (and light) scans on their targets. Full version scans may trigger the target's defense systems, so it would be best if you'll stay away from those options. Here's a screenshot of the dropdown menu:

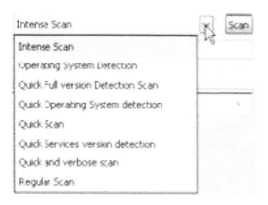

Hit the "Scan" button and wait for the results. Here's a sample:

	Port	Protocol	State	Service	Version
●	22	tcp	open	ssh	
●	24	tcp	open	priv-mail	
●	53	tcp	open	domain	
●	80	tcp	open	http	
●	111	tcp	open	rpcbind	
●	3306	tcp	open	mysql	

As you can see, Nmap can detect the ports and services present in the target.

Banner Grabbing

In this phase, you'll get more information about the target's ports and services. Hackers use telnet to get accomplish this task. The following exercise will help you to understand this phase:

Access your computer's terminal (if you're a Mac user) or command prompt (if you're a Windows user).

> Important Note: If your operating system is Windows Vista, you have to install telnet manually. Here's what you need to do:

Go to the Control Panel and click on "Programs and Features".

Hit "Turn Windows features on or off" and choose "Telnet Client".

Hit the OK button.

The screen will show you a confirmation message.

Choose an open port. For this exercise, let's assume that you selected port 21 (i.e. the FTP port). To determine the FTP software used by the target, use this syntax: telnet <the target's URL> <the port number you selected>

For the present example, the command that you should run is:

telnet www.target-site.com 21

Your computer will determine the type and version of the selected port. Then, it will show the information on your screen. Here's a sample:

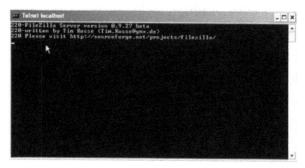

Looking for Weaknesses

Now that you have some information about the port's software, you may start looking for an available "exploit" (i.e. a tool used for hacking computers/networks). If an exploit is available, you may use it on the targeted service and assume total control. If no exploit is available, on the other hand, you have to work on a different port.

Here are the exploit databases commonly used by hackers:

osvdb

exploit-db

SecurityFocus

Many hackers look for another port when they don't have an exploit for the current one. However, you can't assume that all hackers will. Some hackers, particularly the experienced ones, will analyze the targeted port, look for weaknesses and create an exploit. Computer hackers refer to newly discovered weaknesses as "0-day." These weaknesses offer the following benefits:

Nobody knows how to fix the weakness. That means you may hack countless websites before the weakness is discovered and fixed.

The discoverer may sell the weakness for a lot of money. People are willing to spend hundreds (or even thousands) of dollars just to get their hands on fresh vulnerabilities.

Discovering network weaknesses and generating an exploit for them shows that you are skilled and knowledgeable. Other hackers will consider you as an expert.

The Most Common Hacking Attacks

Prior to discussing actual network penetrations, let's talk about two of the most popular hacking attacks.

DoS – This is the abbreviation for "Denial-of-Service." With this attack, the hacker wants to take down the server. That means legitimate users won't be able to access the network or use the affected service/s. Most of the time, hackers accomplish this by sending an endless stream of data to the target network. This tactic forces the network to spend all available resources. Once the resources have been consumed, nobody will be able to use the network.

Buffer Overflow – Hackers also refer to this attack as "BoF." Buffer overflow attacks occur when a computer program tries to save loads of data into a storage area (also known as "buffer"). Since buffers have limited storage capacity, the excess data goes to other areas. When this happens, the hacker may flood the network with malicious codes.

Two Types of Exploits

Hackers divide exploits into two categories, namely:

Local Exploits – These exploits require the hacker to access the target computer physically. In general, attackers use this exploit to escalate their access privileges on the machine or network. Simply put, you may use a local exploit to have admin privileges over your target.

Remote Exploits – These exploits are similar to their local counterparts. The only difference is that hackers may run a remote exploit without accessing the target physically; thus, remote exploits are safer in comparison to local ones.

Important Note: Most of the time, hackers use both types of exploits in their attacks. For instance, you may use a remote exploit to gain ordinary privileges. Then, you can use a local exploit to have admin access to the target. This approach allows you to control a machine or network completely.

Penetrating

This section will teach you how hackers penetrate their targets.

Programming Languages

While practicing your hacking skills, you'll discover that hackers use different programming languages in creating exploits. The following list shows the most popular programming languages today:

PHP – You'll find lots of PHP exploits these days. When writing an exploit using this language, you have to start the code with "<?php" and end it with "?>". Let's assume that you want to inflict some temporary damages to an FTP server. If you'll use the Exploit-DB database, you will find this exploit:

https://www.exploit-db.com/exploits/39082/

Here are the steps you need to take to when hacking a target:

Install the PHP language into your computer. You may visit this <u>site</u> to get PHP for free.

Copy the PHP code from Exploit-DB and paste it onto a word processor. Save the file as "exploit.php".

Go to the 13th line of the exploit and enter your target's IP address. Save the modified file into your computer's PHP directory (i.e. the directory that contains the PHP .exe file).

Access your computer's command prompt. Then, run the CD (i.e. change directory) command and specify the location of the PHP directory.

Type "php exploit.php" and press the Enter key.

Your computer will launch a DoS attack against your target. The attack will only stop once you close the command prompt.

Test the effects of your attack. To do this, visit the target website and click on the tabs/buttons. If the attack is successful, the website will lag and experience unusually long load times. After some time, the site may go offline completely.

Perl – This language is as easy and simple as PHP. To use this programming language, you should:

Visit this site: http://www.activestate.com/activeperl. Then, download and install the right version of Perl.

Look for an exploit that you can use. For this book, let's assume that you want to attack a WinFTP server using this exploit:

https://www.exploit-db.com/exploits/36861/

Modify the code by entering the required information (e.g. the URL of your target, the port you want to attack, etc.). Then, copy it onto a text file and save the document as "exploit.pl".

Access the command prompt. Specify the location of the Perl file using the Change Directory command.

Type "perl exploit.pl" to run the exploit. The program will launch a DoS attack against your target. Just like in the previous example, this exploit will only stop once you close the command prompt window.

Chapter 5: Penetration Testing

Penetration Testing is a legal attempt to detect, probe and attack computer networks. Most of the time, this kind of test is initiated by the network owners. They want hackers to run exploits against the network being tested, so they can measure and improve its defences.

When conducting a Penetration Test, you should look for weaknesses in the target and conduct POC (i.e. proof of concept) attacks. A POC attack is a hacking attack designed to prove a discovered weakness. Effective Penetration Tests always produce detailed suggestions for fixing the problems that were discovered during the procedure. Simply put, Penetration Testing protects networks and computers from future hacking attacks.

The Four-Step Model of Penetration Testing

Hackers divide Penetration Testing into four distinct steps. This approach helps them to identify the things they need to do at any point of the process. Let's discuss each step:

Reconnaissance

During this step, the hacker needs to gather information about the target. It helps the hacker to identify the tools and programs that he needs to use. If the hacker wants to make sure that he will succeed, he must spend considerable time in the Reconnaissance step.

Scanning

This step has two parts, which are:

Port Scanning – You've learned about this topic in an earlier chapter. Basically, port scanning is the process of detecting the available ports in the target. Ports serve as communication lines – once you have detected and controlled it, you will be able to interact with the target network.

Vulnerability Scanning – In this process, you will search for existing vulnerabilities within the network. You'll use the discovered ports (see above) to reach and exploit the vulnerabilities.

Exploitation

Since you have gathered information about the target, scanned the network's ports and searched for existing vulnerabilities, you are now ready to conduct the "actual hacking." This step involves various tools, codes and techniques (some of which have been discussed earlier). The main goal of this phase is to gain admin access over the network.

Maintaining Access

This is the last part of the 4-step model. Obviously, establishing admin access over the target isn't enough. You have to maintain that access so you can conduct other attacks against the system and prove the existence of weaknesses. To accomplish this task, white hat hackers use backdoor programs and remote exploits.

Conclusion

Thank you again for downloading this book!

I hope this book was able to help you learn the basics of hacking.

The next step is to practice your hacking skills and write your own exploits. By doing so, you will become an elite hacker in no time.

Finally, if you enjoyed this book, then I'd like to ask you for a favor, would you be kind enough to leave a review for this book on Amazon? It'd be greatly appreciated!

Please leave a review for this book on Amazon!

Thank you and good luck!